REPUBLIC EARTH

BY DANIEL WHITE

www.republicearth.org

FRONT IMAGE

Republic Earth Flag by Andrew White 2014

Printed and bound in Australia by BookPOD

ISBN: 978-0-646-92524-0

CONTENTS

PROLOGUE

Ω

'Let us not wallow in the valley of despair. I say to you today my friends, so even though we face the difficulties of today and tomorrow, I still have a dream. It is a dream deeply rooted in the American dream.

I have a dream that one day this nation will rise up and live out the true meaning of its creed: "We hold these truths to be self-evident, that all men are created equal." '[1]

Martin Luther King

On 28 August 1963 Martin Luther King delivered his famous 'I Have a Dream Speech' in which he explained his dream of ending racism as part of an egalitarian United States. His eloquent words still resonate today and will live on for eras, but it is time for a broader vision of this dream. The dream for the 21st century for a generation of young Millennials is to use the brilliance of democracy to capture the imagination of all people living around the world. The Industrial Revolution and now the digital revolution have led to immense changes in our daily lives and have created a more globally interconnected world. Humanity has benefited from both

---

[1] Martin Luther King Jr, 'I Have a Dream' 28 August 1963, viewed 16 August 2014 <http://www.americanrhetoric.com/speeches/mikihaveadream.htm>

revolutions in many different ways but many challenges for humanity lie ahead, like our global response to the adverse effects of climate change, and continuing to deal with the main economic concerns of people who are seeking the opportunity to be able to find work and have a level of security for both themselves and their families. In order to be able to address humanity's challenges in the future it is vital that we realise the full potential of democracy by coming together for the common good and creating a new egalitarian dream called Republic Earth.

Republic Earth is an educational, social, political, economic and technological ideology that aims at the establishment of a full global democracy that values all aspects of humanity around the world. Republic Earth primarily aims to build a global online democracy using the technology of the digital revolution, as soon everyone on Earth will be connected if they wish to be. Republic Earth also aims to increase the interconnection of peoples around the world in such a way that fosters a meaningful retention of all human cultures and languages throughout the globe. Republic Earth appreciates that in the coming years people will increasingly reach, and relate to, people far beyond our own borders and language groups, sharing ideas, doing business and building genuine relationships. Republic Earth will also encourage people to be democratically active and creative, while also celebrating the creativity of humanity. Republic Earth believes that as more people come online, they will quite suddenly have access to almost all the world's information in one place, in their own language, and the collective benefit of sharing human knowledge and creativity will be exponential. The origins of Republic Earth are inspired by Australia and cities like Melbourne and Sydney, which have developed robust multicultural societies that have been enriched by greater diversity. According to Sacha Payne, 'More than a quarter of Melbourne's population was born overseas with Victorians speaking more than 260 languages and dialects, coming from 200 different countries and sharing 135 different faiths.[2] The goal of Republic Earth is to encourage a global proliferation in awareness of other cultures and peoples around the world for the greater benefit of humanity.

The Republic Earth concept builds on concepts and educational principles that originated in the classical world and the Renaissance, social principles promoted in multicultural societies, democratic principles that originated in Ancient Greece, economic principles promoted during the New Deal and technological principles promoted during the recent IT revolution. In doing so, the Republic Earth ideology seeks to create new global educational, political, social, economic and technological principles and institutions for the 21st century. Moreover, the Republic Earth ideology encourages Australia as being the country to lead this concept and sees cities like Melbourne potentially becoming a Global Capital in the 21st century, sharing the burden with other cities like New York in defending democracy and promoting diversity. The Republic Earth concept also aims to assist Australia in becoming a modern prototype republic and aims to help it establish an Australian head of state; but the Republic Earth concept will hopefully broaden out to other countries and gain momentum worldwide, with valuing democracy and the fullness of humanity as the keys to long-lasting peace and enjoyment for all peoples on planet Earth. An editorial in *The Age* (2011) has pointed out 'one thing that distinguishes Australia as a nation is that it does not owe its origin to war, revolution or civil

---

[2]   Sacha Payne, 'Australian cities consistently outrank other places in global liveability ratings', viewed 25 August 2014.
http://www.sbs.com.au/news/article/2014/08/23/does-multiculturalism-make-city-more-liveable>

upheaval'.[3] However, we also note the poor treatment of the indigenous population and that Australia is yet to establish its independence as a republic. The intent is that the Republic Earth concept will give Australia a broader context and greater sense of direction and purpose in fulfilling its dream of becoming a republic that is meaningful and purposeful for all of humanity.

This book will begin by looking at the genesis of Republic Earth. It will then explain the twin pillars of Republic Earth, which are democracy and the republic. It will then examine the democratic revolution that needs to occur to make Republic Earth official before explaining in detail what the Republic Earth ideology entails. Finally, this book will show how the Republic Earth concept can be used to assist Australia in its transition to becoming a Republic of Australia with an Australian head of state.

---

[3] 'Write indigenous people into the constitution', *The Age* 12 December 2011, viewed 12 December 2011 < http://www.theage.com.au/opinion/editorial/write-indigenous-people-into-the-constitution-20111211-1opmp.html>

CHAPTER I: GENESIS OF REPUBLIC EARTH

Ω

'We must be the great arsenal of democracy.'[4]

Franklin Delano Roosevelt

The imagined global democratic community of Republic Earth is not yet official, but the Republic Earth ideology has ancient roots that go back to Ancient Greece and Ancient Rome. In modern times the genesis of this notion of Republic Earth is traced back to the 1930s when aviation opened the world to more people.

On Sunday 30 April 1939, the President of the United States, Franklin Delano Roosevelt, stood before an audience of over 200,000 people in Flushing Meadows, Queens, just east of New York City, and steadied himself at the podium. His role that day was to open formally the 1939 New York World's Fair. The theme of the Fair was 'Building the World of Tomorrow' and during its two seasons of activity in 1939 and 1940 it attracted 45 million visitors from around the world. In his speech to open the World's Fair Roosevelt, in the first presidential speech to be televised, said:

'All who come to this World's Fair in New York and to the Exposition in San Francisco will, I need not tell them, receive the heartiest of welcomes.

---

[4] Franklin Delano Roosevelt, 'Fireside Chat' 29 December 1940, viewed 16 August 2014
<https://www.mtholyoke.edu/acad/intrel/woprldwar2/arsenal.htm>

They will find that the eyes of the US are fixed on the future. Yes, our wagon is still hitched to a star. But it is a star of friendship, a star of progress for mankind, a star of greater happiness and less hardship, a star of international goodwill, and, above all, a star of peace. May the months to come carry us forward in the rays of that eternal hope.'[5]

In making this speech and opening the World's Fair, Franklin Roosevelt, who had been inspired by former US Presidents Teddy Roosevelt and Woodrow Wilson (who founded the League of Nations), unknowingly provided a new hope and direction for the world that was to plant the seeds of a new republic – a type of republic further envisioned by American architect and futurist Buckminster Fuller, called 'Republic Earth'. Buckminster Fuller's Republic Earth concept aimed to develop an 'immediate democracy' of multiple referendums by phone.[6] Now, with the invention of the internet, this Republic Earth concept has the possibility of becoming a reality.

President Franklin Delano Roosevelt is arguably one of the greatest politicians to have ever lived. During times of economic hardship and war Roosevelt provided the 'security and opportunities' that both Americans and peoples across the world actually needed. When he came to power in 1933 the United States was fully immersed in the Great Depression, but Roosevelt provided hope and a New Deal and by 1945 America was the

---

[5] Franklin Delano Roosevelt, 'Opening of the New York World's Fair' 30 April
     1939, viewed 16 August 2014
     <http://www.presidency.ucsb.edu/ws/?pid=15755
[6] The Design-Science Revolution of R. Buckminister Fuller Outlined and
     Explained by Libby Hubbard viewed on 2 February 2012 at
     <http://www.lovolution.net/MainPages/essays/FullerEssay/fuller.htm>

strongest economic force on the planet. But his signature achievement was defending democracy against fascism and seeking to bring the world together for the common good by creating institutions like the United Nations that still remain today rather than seeking to divide the world in the manner of Adolf Hitler. By 1941 there were only 11 democracies, and Franklin Roosevelt worried that it might not be possible to shield 'the great flame of democracy from the blackout of barbarism'.[7] In this hour of weakness for democracy Roosevelt showed tremendous leadership during WWII and ensured that democracy survived.

If Roosevelt had an arch nemesis, it must have been Adolf Hitler. On Sunday 30 April 1939 Adolf Hitler was not trying to bring the world together by opening a World's Fair. Instead, his Nazi Party was instituting a law to force landlords to evict Jews from their homes.[8] For all the cruel and inhumane political leaders there have been in human history there are few more barbaric than Adolf Hitler. The demise of the Weimar Republic, Hitler's destruction of Germany's democracy and the rise of fascism was one of the world's greatest atrocities. Such events provide us with many lessons, but most importantly we must not become unhitched from Roosevelt's star of democracy, a star of international goodwill and a star of peace. Roosevelt's vision for a united nations is now largely the inspiration for a democratic Republic Earth.

---

[7]   Franklin Delano Roosevelt, 'Address at the Annual Dinner of the White House Correspondents' Associations 15 March 1941, viewed 16 August 2014 <http://www.presidency.ucsb.edu/ws/?pid=16089>

[8]   '20 century – Jews evicted from homes', viewed 16 August 2014, <http://www.precden.com/timelines/67045-20-cenury>

CHAPTER II: DEMOCRACY

Ω

'Democracy is something one must nourish all one's life, if
it is to remain alive and strong.'[9]

Aung San Suu Kyi

Democracy forms the first pillar of Republic Earth. Democracy is humanity's finest achievement because democracy reflects the reality of human existence – that we are complex creatures and often impotent in the face of our own nature. A democratic society is the expression of a multitude of lives and voices, and democracy is a continual act of communal creativity – and the energy required to keep creating and keep democracy vibrant is immense, as are the forces like fear that have raged and continue to rage against it. Democracy historian Roger Osborne puts it best by saying in his book, *Of the People by the People: A New History of Democracy*, that:

> 'More than all the paintings and sculptures on Earth, more than
> all the poems, plays and novels, and more than every scientific
> and technological invention put together, democracy shows
> humanity at its most creative and innovative; democracy is a

---

[9]   Aung San Suu Kyi, *Freedom from Fear: And Other Writings,* (Penguin Books, London, 1991), 13

continual, collective enterprise that binds us together while allowing us to live individually.'[10]

The world is changing; existing democracies face new challenges, including economic gridlock and the possibility of catastrophic climate change, while people of different cultures are seeking to build emerging democracies in their own lands. During this time of change in a more globally interconnected world there is an opportunity for humanity to truly embrace democracy. The history of democracy can offer some guidance for the future. Firstly, democracies must continually create new ways of working if they are to survive. Secondly, democracies must have faith in their own people and at no stage deny the voice of the people to truly be expressed. Each person's voice will eventually fade and be rounded by history, but in the 21st century it is vital that everybody's creative voice is heard as that is when dreams are made. While democracy endures there is hope; without democracy the world is bereft, with tyranny of the few over the many.

What is democracy? Democracy is an idea that first appears about 507 BC under the Athenian leader Cleisthenes. Cleisthenes abolished the four ancient tribes of Athens. He saw these tribes as a major source of power, through systems of patronage and deference, for the leading families. According to Osborne, in their place Cleisthenes brought in ten new tribes, organised so that the membership of each equally represented districts, or demos, on the coast, in the countryside and in the city.[11] This not only dissolved the old power bases, but brought people from different parts of the polis into contact with each other, reinforcing a sense of communal

---

[10] Roger Osborne, *Of the People By the People: A New History of Democracy* (Bodley Head, London, 2011), 1.

[11] Ibid, 14.

identity. This political redistribution lasted, with minor alterations, for 700 years. Cleisthenes developed a horizontal division of society containing members of every class rather than a vertical division of society based on wealth.

Demokratia means 'rule of the people' and is the opposite to aristocracy which means 'ruled by an elite'. The Pnyx is a rocky outcrop on a sacred hill opposite the Acropolis where the first known democratic gathering took place. On the Pnyx the Ekklesia of about 5,000 Athenian men would assemble to vote and members would gather on the rock and raise hands. All adult citizens were able to vote except slaves, women and foreigners.[12] Democracy claims to give every citizen a voice and to restrain the power of tyrants. Democracy in ancient Athens gave birth to a new kind of politics in which the conflicts in society were brought out into the open, and debated in the council and the assembly and contained within those forums. This was such a breathtaking innovation in human affairs that it took decades for Greek writers to begin to comprehend its significance.

During the Enlightenment and the French and American Revolutions new democratic ideas came to the forefront. Italian Renaissance thinkers like Leonardo Bruni contended that cities can only be great once their people are free, and this means free from monarchs, princes and tyrants. French Enlightenment thinkers like Rousseau, Montesquieu and Voltaire came up with concepts like liberty, equality and fraternity that sought to break down aristocratic rule and give power to the middle class. The views of Scottish Enlightenment philosophers like David Hume and Adam Smith on free will, civil government, liberty of the press and economics provided

---

[12] "The Ekklesia (Citizens' Assembly), viewed 16 August 2014 <http://www.agathe.gr/democracy/the_ekklesia.html>

new ideas for civilisation. In particular, the global reach of Adam Smith's moral and political reasoning and his belief that all humans are born with similar potential promoted new democratic ideas of equality. American Founding Fathers like Jefferson, Adams, Washington and Franklin fused concepts of democracy and the republic together via a constitution to ensure power rested with the people.

Democracy over the years has become a truly universal value and despite its European heritage democratic principles have had a history in Asia, the Middle East and in Africa. For example, former South Korean President Kim Dae Jung has often noted and celebrated Asia's 'rich heritage of democracy-oriented philosophies and traditions'.[13] According to democracy expert Larry Diamond in his book, *The Spirit of Democracy*, 'These include the works of the Chinese philosopher Meng-tzu, who identified a right of the people to overthrow a king "in the name of heaven" if he did not provide good government, and the Korean religion of Tonghak, whose "ideas inspired and motivated nearly half a million peasants in 1894 to revolt against exploitation by feudalistic government internally and imperialistic forces externally".'[14] One can also look to Sun Yat-sen who was the first President and founding father of the Republic of China back in 1912, as he was a democratic revolutionary who played an instrumental role in the overthrow of the Qing dynasty. This insight into the history of both China and South Korea shows evidence of a democratic tradition of 'opposition to despotism' and 'suspicion of state power'. Diamond,

---

[13] Larry Diamond, The Spirit of Democracy: The Struggle to Build Free Societies Throughout the World, (Times Books/henry Holt & Company, New York, 2008), 29.

[14] Ibid.

meanwhile, notes that 'the Indian experience of religious tolerance under a Muslim empire is but one example of a long historical tradition of tolerance and progress within the Islamic societies of the Middle East'.[15] Finally, in Africa uprisings in Ancient Egypt and Ghana's Independence in 1957 reveal democracy's universal value throughout the world.

Democracy had its challenges in the 20th century as a result of the First and Second World Wars but after Portugal became a democracy in 1976, President Ferdinand Marcos was overthrown in the Philippines in 1986 and Cold War ended in 1991 there was an unprecedented political boom for democracy that lasted until the end of the century. In April 1974, dictatorship, not democracy, was the way of the world. Barely a quarter of independent states chose their governments through competitive, free and fair elections. However, with the overthrow of the dictatorship in Portugal in 1974, the third wave of democratisation began with both Portugal and Spain becoming democracies, which influenced the scene in Latin America with the Dominican Republic, Peru and Ecuador all becoming democracies by 1980. Despite these important changes, the global democratic trend remained quite limited until the overthrow of President Ferdinand Marcos in the Philippines in 1986 that triggered the winds of democratic change throughout Asia with South Korea becoming a democracy in 1987 and Taiwan in 1996. Even China was affected by the democratic change sweeping the region, as according to Diamond 'thousands of students and intellectuals came to Beijing's Tiananmen Square in April 1989 to mourn the sudden death of the reformist general secretary of the Communist party, Hu Yaobang'.[16] However, the end of the Cold War and the break-up

---

[15] Ibid, 30.
[16] Ibid, 45.

of Yugoslavia and the Soviet empire led to three-fifths of all world states becoming democracies at an astonishing speed.

Nowadays across the world democracy has become a desirable end - both for citizens who want their voice to be heard, and for leaders who need its legitimacy in order to enter the international system. According to the '2012 Democracy Index' compiled by the Economist Intelligence Unit, there are 167 so called democratic countries, of which 166 are sovereign states and 165 are United Nations member states.[17] Of these 167 democratic countries, there are 25 full democracies, 54 flawed democracies, 37 hybrid regimes and 51 authoritarian regimes.[18] Arguably the greatest failure of democratic governments in our time has been the surrender of power to the international financial system in return for short-term prosperity for their leaders and their nations. The traders of the Agora once shrank before the power of the assembly but now our leaders must bend to the will of the markets - the Pnyx bending its knee to the Agora. This will change, but only by making the world more democratic not less. Making South Africa more democratic is what Nelson Mandela believed in when he stated on 20 April 1964 that:

'During my lifetime, I have dedicated myself to this struggle of the African people. I have fought against white domination, and I have fought against black domination. I have cherished the ideal of a democratic and free society in which all persons live together in harmony and with equal

---

[17] 'Democracy Index 2012: Democracy at a standstill' A report from the Economist Intelligence Unit, viewed 16 August 2014, <https://portoncv.gov.cv/dhub/porton.por_global.open_file?p_doc_id=1034 >

[18] Ibid.

opportunities. It is an ideal which I hope to live for and to achieve. But if needs be, it is an ideal for which I am prepared to die.'[19]

To Nelson Mandela's credit his dream has become a reality and it is because of his dedication to his dream that there was so much outpouring of love and admiration for him as a leader around the world when he passed away in 2013.

In the 21st century many democratic challenges do remain. For instance, most countries whose economies are dominated by oil are not democracies. Since 2000, democracy has been extinguished by the undemocratic actions of elected presidents in Russia and Venezuela, by a royal coup in Nepal and by massive electoral fraud in Nigeria in 2003. And several powerful authoritarian countries – such as China, Belarus and Uzbekistan, as well as democratic countries like Turkey – have been narrowing the space for dissent and opposition. China still remains the biggest obstacle to democracy in the 21st century. The Chinese Communist state is still a brutal one, officially executing somewhere between five thousand and twelve thousand people each year, including democratic dissenters. According to a recent essay by *The Economist*, 'What is Wrong with Democracy': 'The Chinese elite argue that their model – tight control by the Communist Party, coupled with a relentless effort to recruit talented people into its upper ranks – is more efficient than democracy and less susceptible to gridlock.'[20] Thus democracy is facing a huge uphill battle to succeed in China. Meanwhile, democracy in the United States has become

---

[19]   Rivonia Trial' 20 April 1964, viewed 16 August 2014,
       <http://www.nelsonmandela.org/content/mini-site/introduction-from-the-book>
[20]   'What's gone wrong with democracy' *The Economist* 1 March 2014, 48.

gridlocked, corrupted by gerrymandering, and infected by special interest groups with large amounts of money behind them, which creates the impression that American democracy is for sale and that the rich have more power than ordinary American citizens. In Europe democratic governments in Greece, Spain and Italy have come under increasing pressure economically for running big structural deficits to give short-term benefits to votes at the expense of long-term investment, the European Parliament is dismissed by many Europeans, and Greece's Golden Dawn is testing how far democracies can tolerate Nazi-style parties. In such a climate there is an opportunity for a country like Australia to use its position, being the first country in the world to be created out of a democratic vote and being the oldest and most stable democracy in the Asia-Pacific region, to cultivate a spirit of democracy around the world in the years ahead to overcome the democratic challenges mentioned above.

In 2014, a huge year for democracy lies ahead as voters will go to the polls in some of the biggest countries of the developing world, including India, Indonesia and Brazil. In the developed world we will hopefully see some improvement in voter turnout during elections as, according to *The Economist*, voter turnout has been falling slowly since the 1970s, from more than 80 per cent to less than 70 per cent by 2011.[21] Fortunately, there are some recent signs that young people are becoming more active through public demonstrations, particularly when issues affect them directly, while the internet has provided a new channel of democratic and community expression. The internet makes it easier to organise and agitate, as with a click of the mouse you can sign a petition and voice your concerns, or organise rallies via social media platforms like Facebook, Twitter and

---

[21]   Ibid, 50.

YouTube that facilitated the Arab Spring and the recent Occupy Wall Street protests to occur. Meanwhile, according to *The Economist*, 'Finland is trying to harness e-democracy: parliament is obliged to consider any citizens' initiative that gains 50,000 signatures'.[22] Hopefully with this democratic spirit in our youth, combined with the internet and e-democracy, it will be possible to create a brand new democratic global community called Republic Earth.

---

[22] Ibid, 52.

CHAPTER III: THE REPUBLIC

Ω

'There is no king or queen bee distinguished from all others, by size or figure or beauty and variety of all colours, in the human hive. No man has yet produced any revelation from heaven in his favour, any divine communication to govern his fellow men. Nature throws us all into this world equal and alike.'[23]

John Adams

The second pillar of Republic Earth is the notion of the republic. The ancient world of Plato, Aristotle, Ploybius, Livy and Plutarch also introduces us to the concept of the republic: a state without a monarch where the people are sovereign. According to Osborne, it is believed that the Roman Republic was founded around 509 BC, with the expulsion of the last king by a combination of powerful families led by Lucius Junius Brutus.[24] The Roman Republic eventually collapsed in 27 BC when the powers of the elite became virtually uncheckable. Power became attached to successful generals like Julius Caesar and Gnaeus Pompeius, resulting in civil wars fought over loyalty to one leader or another. In 44 BC Julius Caesar's grandiloquence provoked a group of conspirators led by Marcus Junius Brutus who were desperate to save the republic from becoming a

---

[23] John Adams, from notes for an oration at Braintree, Massachusetts, diary entry of 10 February 1772 in L H Butterfield, ed, *Diary & Autobiography of John Adams,* 57-58.

[24] Osborne, Of the People, By the People, 25.

monarchy. But Caesar's assassination brought about another power struggle that ended in 27 BC when Octavian was named by the senate Augustus, or 'the revered one', and the Roman Republic gave way to the Roman Empire.

Currently in the modern world 135 of the world's 206 sovereign states use the word 'republic' as part of their official names.[25] However, not all republics are 'full democracies', which allow the people to be fully sovereign. According to The Economist Intelligence Unit's Democracy Index there are only 25 full democracies and of those there are only 13 republics in the truest form of the word.[26] (The 13 republics are: Iceland, Switzerland, Finland, Austria, Ireland, Germany, Malta, Czech Republic, Uruguay, Mauritius, South Korea, United States of America and Costa Rica.) Despite all our talk of democracy and republics, it is clear that in most so called 'democratic' countries in the world we do not have rule by the people for the people and in most so called 'republics' the sovereignty is not fully in the hands of the people. This is a reality that needs to change, as everybody's democratic voice deserves to be heard in a community where the people are sovereign.

---

[25] 'Republic', viewed 16 August 2014, http://en.m.wikipedia.org/wiki/Republic>
[26] 'Democracy Index 2012'.

CHAPTER IV: THE DEMOCRATIC REVOLUTION

Ω

'The Revolution was effected before the war
commenced. The Revolution was in the minds and hearts
of the people. This radical change in the principles,
opinions, sentiments and affections of the people was the
real American Revolution.'[27]

John Adams

In order to create a Republic Earth, a democratic revolution is needed in the way we think about the world. This democratic revolution does not need to involve war or bloodshed, but simply needs people around the world to believe that creating a democratic global community called Republic Earth will benefit them. Two great technological revolutions have occurred in recent times, the Industrial Revolution and the digital revolution. Both these technological revolutions were honoured during the London 2012 Olympic Opening Ceremony. Danny Boyle, the director of the ceremony, aimed to show the greatness of Britain, and said that:

'At some point in their histories most nations experience a revolution that changes everything about them. The United Kingdom had a revolution that

---

[27] Kelly Gneiting, 'The Real American Revolution', a quote by John Adams 1818', viewed 16 August 2014
<http://www.independentamericanparty.org/2011/09/the-real-american-revolution-a-quote-by-john-adams/>

changed the whole of human existence. In 1709 Abraham Darby smelted iron in a blast furnace, using coke. And so began the Industrial Revolution. Out of Abraham's Shropshire furnace flowed molten metal. Out of his genius flowed the mills, looms, engines, weapons, railways, ships, cities, conflicts and prosperity that built the world we live in. In November 1990 another Briton sparked another revolution – equally far reaching – a revolution we're still experiencing. The digital revolution was sparked by Tim Berners-Lee's amazing gift to the world – the World Wide Web. This, he said, is for everyone.'[28]

In light of the democratic deficit that exists in the world at present and in light of the lack of devotion to what a republic actually represents, it is important to embody Danny Boyle's spirit and create a democratic revolution that is for everyone – to create a democratic republic that is for everyone to enjoy right around the world, as Tim Berners-Lee's invention of the World Wide Web sparked a global communications revolution that has left no part of our lives untouched.

In December 1862, Abraham Lincoln gave his second annual address to Congress. He was writing one month before he signed the Emancipation Proclamation, and in his message he urged Congress to see the situation they faced with fresh eyes. He said this:

'The dogmas of the quiet past are inadequate to the stormy present. The occasion is piled high with difficulty. As our case is new, so we must think

---

[28]   Danny Boyle, 'Summer Olympics Opening Ceremony 2012', viewed 16 August 2014
http://en.m.wikipedia.org/wiki/2012_Summer_Olympics_Opening_Ceremony>

anew and act anew. We must disenthrall ourselves and then we shall save our country.'[29]

What disenthrall meant was that we all live our lives guided by ideas to which we are devoted but which may no longer be true or relevant to our times. We are hypnotised or enthralled by them. To move forward we have to shake free of them. This is what we must do now. We can no longer be enthralled and accept that everything is right in the world when most people's democratic voice is either non-existent or ignored. We must disenthrall ourselves and think anew and act anew. We must realise that we have an obligation to carry out as part of the digital revolution, a democratic revolution that strengthens the principle of democracy and in so doing creates a Republic Earth.

---

[29]   Abraham Lincoln, Annual Message to Congress – 1 December 1862, viewed 16 August 2014
http://www.abrahamlincolnonline.org/lincoln/speeches/congress.htm>

CHAPTER V: REPUBLIC EARTH

Ω

'We are not going to be able to operate our Spaceship
Earth successfully nor for much longer unless we see it as
a whole spaceship and our fate as common. It has to be
everybody or nobody.'[30]

Buckminster Fuller

Republic Earth is an education, social, political, economic and
technological ideology that aims at the establishment of a full global
democracy that values all aspects of humanity around the world. Republic
Earth is secular and will adhere to the United Nations Universal Declaration
on Human Rights. The Republic Earth ideology believes in pluralism and
aims to increase the interconnection of peoples around the world in such a
way that fosters a soulful retention of all human cultures and languages
throughout the globe. In doing so, the Republic Earth ideology will help to
celebrate the creativity of humanity.

Republic Earth is an 'imagined community'. 'Imagined communities' is a
concept coined by Benedict Anderson.[31] An imagined community is
different from an actual community because it is not (and, for practical

---

[30] Buckminister Fuller, 'Everything I Know' 1975, viewed 16 August 2014
      <http://spacecollective.org/A0013237932294/1082/we-are-not-going-to-be-
      able-to-operate-spaceship-earth-successfully>
[31] Benedict Anderson, Imagined Communities: Reflections on the Origins &
      Spread of Nationalism, (Verso, London, 1988), 1

reasons, cannot be) based on everyday face-to-face interaction between its members. For example, Anderson believes that a nation is a socially constructed community, imagined by the people who perceive themselves as part of that group. Within the 'imagined community' called Republic Earth there are 7.099 billion people, between 6,000 and 7,000 languages and 370 million indigenous people living in 90 countries around the world.

The world has become globally interconnected and flat at the start of the 21st century. This notion of 'The World is Flat' was coined by New York Times columnist Thomas Friedman, as he said that 'it is my contention that the fall of the Berlin Wall, the rise of the PC, Netscape, workflow, outsourcing, offshoring, uploading, insourcing, supply-chaining, informing, and the steroids [of these flattening forces created a world that is now flat]'.[32] Republic Earth aims to create a global online democratic community in the flat world that we now inhabit and live in. Moreover, Eric Schmidt and Jared Cohen in their book, *The New Digital Age*, conclude that 'by 2025, the majority of the world's population will, in one generation, have gone from having virtually no access to unfiltered information to accessing all the world's information through a device that fits in the palm of your hand. If the current pace of technological innovation is maintained, most of the projected eight billion people on Earth will be online [by 2025]'.[33] Republic Earth believes 2025 will be a crucial year, as not only will every person on the planet be globally interconnected via the internet, but the majority of Chinese will have to some degree entered the middle

---

[32] Thomas L Friedman, The World Is Flat: The Globalized World in the Twenty First Century, (Penguin Books, London, 2006), 204.

[33] Eric Schmidt & Jared Cohen, *The New Digital Age: Transforming Nations, Business & Our Lives,* (Vintage Books, New York, 2014), 4.

class and this more informed Chinese society may allow democracy to prosper in China. According to Diamond, 'Having gotten much of the material base of a better life, they will want more: justice, dignity, accountability, voice. ... Chinese rulers would have to contend with a larger, more resourceful, and better networked civil society than what existed during the last democratic uprising, in 1989.'[34] Gene Sharp's book, *From Dictatorship to Democracy*, makes it clear that due to the human dimension some dictatorships have 'proved unable to withstand the concerted, political, economic, and social defiance of the people', and subsequently using Sharp's 198 methods of non-violent protest and persuasion the Chinese middle class may lead China to become a democracy.[35] Even Hillary Clinton has noted in her recent book, *Hard Choices*, that 'the internet has become the public space of the 21st century, the world's town square', which showcases that Republic Earth could become a reality.[36] In light of this extraordinary reality of super empowered individuals by 2025 and a growing Chinese middle class, the establishment of a global online democracy involving all people on the planet will be possible and thus Republic Earth aims to ensure each person's voice is allowed to be heard in this globally interconnected world.

It could be argued that educationally the Republic Earth is already in action, gaining momentum and captivating young people around the globe. For example, academics like Michael J Sandel, political philosopher from Harvard, and Jeffrey Sachs, director of the Earth Institute at Columbia

---

[34] Diamond, The Spirit of Democracy, 233.

[35] Gene Sharp, From Dictatorship to Democracy: A Conceptual Framework for Liberation, (Serpent's Tail, London, 1993), 1

[36] Hillary Clinton, *Hard Choices: A Memoir*, (Simon & Schuster, Australia, 2014), 551.

University, are now conducting 'global classrooms' whereby students are asked to engage in the key political debates of the day and to value the opinions of other students on the screen who are sitting in a different country with a different perspective on the world.[37] The message here is that education is increasingly becoming more effective and accessible to all young people in the world, if they have access to cheap communications technology. The key now is to ensure that all children throughout the world receive a sound education that not only provides them with the essential skills and knowledge for life but also exposes them to all facets of human endeavour and encourages the development of some form of expertise. Republic Earth also agrees with Ken Robinson in that education has three main roles: 'personal, cultural and economic. Individually, education has a role to develop individual talents and sensibilities. Culturally, education has a role to deepen one's understanding of the world. Economically, education has a role to provide the skills required to earn a living and be economically productive'.[38]

Socially, the goal of Republic Earth is to build on the success of multicultural countries like Australia and to continue to grow awareness of cultures from other countries around the world. The Republic Earth concept does not want to see cultures and languages be lost. Rather, Republic Earth wishes that people begin to have a higher appreciation of other cultures and peoples in an ever changing and highly interconnected world, and in doing so hopefully see the fullness of humanity be protected

---

[37] Michael Sandel, Justice: What's The Right Thing To Do?, (Penguin Books, London, 2010), 1; Jeffrey Sachs 2011, The Price of Civilization: Economics and Ethics after the Fall, (Random House, London, 2011), 258.

[38] Ken Robinson, *Out of Our Minds : Learning to be Creative,* (Capstone Publishing Ltd, UK, 2011), 67

for future generations. In particular, the Republic Earth concept supports cities like Melbourne holding international sporting and artistic festivals, which foster a greater appreciation of the talents of people from all parts of the world. The Republic Earth concept would like cities like Melbourne to add a democratic component to each festival, for example, to work out which is the best film in the world for that particular year during its International Film Festival and which is the best comedian in the world for that particular year during its International Comedy Festival. Voting doesn't just have to be political but can be a fun social pastime as well.

Politically, the Republic Earth ideology builds on democratic principles developed in Ancient Greece and supports democratic activists, like those in the Arab Spring, Burmese opposition leader Aung San Suu Kyi and her supporters, and former Soviet President Mikhail Gorbachev, who have continued to commit to peace and democracy in such a way that inspires young people to campaign for greater democracy, not less, throughout the world. In so doing, democracy has to become a way of life. The Republic Earth concept also encourages democratic countries to appreciate political developments in other like-minded democratic countries and hopes that countries like Australia will stand up and support fledgling democracies and become a strong branch in the tree of democracy. Democracy is in many ways organic like a tree and without looking after it and nurturing it, it will come under threat and may face extinction. The remedy for the ills of democracy is more democracy. Accordingly, the Republic Earth ideology aims at the establishment of a full global democracy with the help of technology and supports the creation of new democratic principles and institutions that build on the work carried out by United Nations bodies at present. Republic Earth believes most human beings want a rules-based democracy that allows people to speak their minds and shape their own and their children's futures. New democratic principles are becoming evident via Sheryl Sandberg's 'Lean In' campaign, which is focused on encouraging women to pursue their ambitions, and Benjamin Barber in his book *If Mayors Ruled the World: Dysfunctional Nations, Rising Cities* calls for a new international institution to be created in the form of a World Assembly of Cities.[39] Republic Earth is also a philosophy of fighting corruption in all places and in all forms, through concepts such as transparency, e.g. the transparency of money.

Economically, the Republic Earth ideology continues to support the maintenance of capitalism as the pre-eminent economic theory but encourages the development of new economic principles and institutions that build on the success of FDR's New Deal. According to Bhide, 'In short, [since the Industrial Revolution] capitalism helped unleash extraordinary growth ... [as] per capita incomes more than doubled, and then, in the twentieth century, increased more than eightfold ... Its capacity to deliver the goods allowed capitalism to prevail over socialism and communism. And although it didn't abolish misery, it produced considerably less of it than its rival system.'[40] However, the recent Global Financial Crisis and the current European Economic Crisis are hallmarks of inherent flaws in the way Wall Street and Global Markets are being run and that they have gone off course. Resurrecting economic principles used during the New Deal that acted in the common good and then adapting and improving them for the 21st century is the way to go to ensure future economic prosperity for humanity. The Republic Earth ideology encourages people throughout the

---

[39] Sheryl Sandberg, *Lean In: Women, Work, And the Will to Lead,* (Random House, New York, 2013), 1; Benjamin Barber, *If Mayors Ruled the World,* (Yale University Press, New York, 2013), 1.

[40] Amar Bhide, *A Call for Judgement: Sensible Finance for a Dynamic Economy,* (Oxford University Press, New York, 2011), 4.

world to start to debate the moral limits of the market, to support the notion of fully guaranteeing all bank deposits and to impose much tighter restrictions on risk-taking by banks, so that capitalism remains balanced and just.

Technologically, the digital revolution has already enabled electronic voting in places like Brazil & Estonia, in a manner similar to internet banking. The internet thus has the possibility of uniting the world in a democracy that would make it Republic Earth. This would almost realise Buckminster Fuller's vision of a worldwide immediate democracy of multiple referendums by phone. The digital revolution and social media tools like Facebook, Twitter and YouTube have meant that people across the world can easily become globally interconnected. Republic Earth aims to build on this momentum to encourage people to become citizens of a brand new online democratic community called Republic Earth by visiting www.republicearth.org. The Republic Earth ideology also hopes that humanity during the next phase of development of technology will focus some of its attention on space exploration.

The central message of the Republic Earth ideology is that we have arrived at a global society where a new generation of young people called Millennials (people aged eighteen to twenty-nine in the year 2010, the group that will shape the world in the next twenty-five years) is increasingly valuing democracy and diversity. Sachs expands on this by noting that 'the Millennials are politically progressive, believing in a larger role for government ... [and] are less likely to be divided or even torn asunder by the culture wars of the boomer generation'.[41] The Republic

---

[41]   Jeffrey Sachs, *The Price of Civilization: Economics and Ethics after the Fall*, (Random House, London, 2011), 254-255.

Earth ideology encourages the Millennials to be inspired and play a role in ensuring peace and prosperity for the future of humanity by using technology to create a worldwide democracy.

One of the great things that has happened during the digital revolution that we are still going through is that we have increasingly become interconnected as a people, especially via social media tools such as Facebook, Twitter and YouTube. If you are a member of the middle class in any part of the world then it is likely that you will be using a social media tool to connect with friends and family members. However, most of the 7 billion citizens in Republic Earth are not in the middle class and thus struggle to connect with the globalised world. The aim of Republic Earth is to use the ideals of the republic and democracy to ensure all 7 billion voices on planet Earth are heard. Republic Earth aims to empower people. Republic Earth aims to treat everyone as equals, with each person's vote being just as important. Everyone, whether they are rich or poor, is an important citizen in Republic Earth. To do this, it helps to grow the middle classes in each country quickly so Republic Earth can become a reality.

For Republic Earth to succeed we need to create a global democracy and grow the world's middle class. The global middle class is expected to double in size by 2035, to as many as 5 billion; however, we need to make sure this happens. We have internet banking so why don't we have democracy on the internet? Democracy has assisted with growing the world's middle class, however the people of the world must mobilise or otherwise risk being enslaved. How will democracy on the internet help you? We are in an aristocratic age and the middle class in the western world is being eroded. According to a study released by the Helsinki-based World Institute for Development Economics Research of the United Nations University (UNU-WIDER), the richest 2 per cent in the world own more than half of the world's wealth, while the poorest 95 per cent of the world's population only own 30 per cent of the world's wealth.[42] During a speech at Knox College, Galesburg, Illinois, US President Barack Obama explained how the middle class is eroding, as he said that:

'In the period after World War II, a growing middle class was the engine of our prosperity. Whether you owned a company, or swept its floors, or worked anywhere in between, this country offered you a basic bargain - a sense that your hard work would be rewarded with fair wages and decent benefits, the chance to buy a home, to save for retirement, and most of all, a chance to hand down a better life for your kids.

But over time, that engine began to stall - and a lot of folks here saw it - that bargain began to fray. Technology made some jobs obsolete. Global competition sent a lot of jobs overseas. It became harder for unions to fight for the middle class. Washington doled out bigger tax cuts to the very wealthy and smaller minimum wage increases for the working poor.

And so what happened was that the link between higher productivity and people's wages and salaries was broken. It used to be that, as companies did better, as profits went higher, workers also got a better deal. And that started changing. So the income of the top 1 per cent nearly quadrupled from 1979 to 2007, but the typical family's incomes barely budged.

And towards the end of those three decades, a housing bubble, credit cards, a churning financial sector was keeping the economy artificially juiced up, so sometimes it papered over some of these long-term trends.

---

[42]   'Pioneering Study Shows Richest Two Per Cent Own Half the World's Wealth', viewed 16 August 2014 <http://www.wider.unu.edu/events/past-events/2006-events/en_GB/05-12-2006>

But by the time I took office in 2009 as your President, we all know the bubble had burst, and it cost millions of Americans their jobs, and their homes, and their savings. And I know a lot of folks in this area were hurt pretty bad. And the decades-long erosion that had been taking place – the erosion of middle-class security – was suddenly laid bare for everybody to see.'[43]

American philosopher Michael J Sandel expands on this eroding of the middle class by suggesting we as a society need to impose some moral limits of the markets if we are going to succeed as a people.[44] In Naomi Klein's book called *The Shock Doctrine* she makes it clear that due to economic policies created by Milton Freedman and his Chicago School of Economics we have witnessed economic shocks and a form of disaster capitalism infect many societies across the world from the 1970s to the present day, leading to a transfer of wealth of unfathomable size.[45] It is a transfer of wealth from public hands, i.e. from governments, collected from regular people in the form of taxes into the hands of the wealthiest corporations and individuals in the world. In light of this transfer of wealth, democracy needs to be revived to grow the world's middle class and ensure their democratic voice is heard, as democracy cannot be stable without a broad and deep middle class.

---

[43] Barack Obama, Remarks by the President on the Economy-Knox College, Galesburg, IL, 24 July 2013, viewed 16 August 2014 <http://m.whitehouse.gov/the-press-office/2013/07/24/remarks-president-ecnomy-knox-college-galesburg,1>

[44] Michael Sandel, *Justice: What's The Right Thing To Do?*, (Penguin Books, London, 2010), 1.

[45] Naomi Klein, The Shock Doctrine: The Rise of Disaster Capitalism, (Penguin Books, London, 2008), 49-50.

Republic Earth believes that to overcome the growing trend of economic inequality and an eroding middle class people should embrace Thomas Piketty's idea of a global progressive tax on capital coupled with a very high level of international financial transparency, as outlined in his book *Capital: In the Twenty-First Century*. According to Piketty, 'the primary purpose of the capital tax is not to finance the social state but to regulate capitalism. The goal is first to stop indefinite increase of inequality of wealth, and second to impose effective regulation on the financial and banking system in order to avoid crises. To achieve these two ends, the capital tax must first promote democratic and financial transparency: there should be clarity about who owns what assets around the world.'[46] Thus to contain the unlimited growth of global inequality of wealth, a capital tax schedule with rates of 0.1 or 0.5 per cent on fortunes under AUS$1 million, 1 per cent on fortunes between AUS$1 million and AUS$5 million, 2 per cent between AUS$5 million and AUS$10 million, and between 5 and 10 per cent for fortunes of several hundred million or several billion Australian dollars should be implemented.

In addition to the eroding of the middle class, democracy is also decaying. The titles of The Economist Intelligence Unit's Democracy Index for 2010, 2011 and 2012, 'Democracy in Retreat', 'Democracy under Stress' and 'Democracy at a Standstill', all reinforce this point.[47] It is our moral duty to revive democracy and be active democratic citizens in our local communities. There is a great FDR story about democracy. When he was

---

[46] Thomas Piketty, *Capital In the Twenty-First Century,* (The Belknap Press of Harvard University Press, Cambridge, 2014), 518.
[47] Democracy Index, viewed 16 August 2014
<http://en.m.wikipedia.org/wiki/Democracy_Index>

visited by some progressive organisation or a union who were promoting some new progressive policy to be added to the New Deal, he would hear them out and then tell them 'now go out there and make me do it'.[48] The great thing was that these progressive groups did go out and protest and in 1937, in a pivotal year for the New Deal, there were 4740 strikes throughout the United States lasting an average of 20 days. Compare this to 2007 when there was only 27 strikes in the United States. The key to progressing democracy is to encourage people to campaign and be active democratic citizens and to not disengage from the political process.

For democracy to be revived it is important that we use the tools of the digital revolution, like smart phones and tablets, to create a globalised democratic community. Multinational companies are generating multinational legal, accounting and engineering firms. The world is going global but our democracy is not. The goal is that hopefully by 2100 each human being in Republic Earth will have access to a smart phone and will be able to vote regularly and be an active democratic citizen. In the 21st century every human being should be encouraged to become part of this hopefully compulsory democratic community.

Republic Earth understands and appreciates the risks of internet voting outlined by David Dill and Barbara Simons from Verified Voting. Republic Earth encourages everyone to read the 'Computer Technologists Statement on Internet Voting' that states election results must be verifiably accurate and outlines the potential risks of internet voting, such as the risks from individual hackers, political parties, international criminal organisations,

---

[48]   'The real story behind "make him do it"' viewed 16 August 2014
      <http://www.wheresourmourmoney.org/the-real-story-behind-make-him-do-it>

hostile foreign governments, denial of service attacks, insider threats or even terrorists.[49] Republic Earth will aim to verify all global votes because without the assurance that the results are verifiably accurate there is an extraordinary and unnecessary risk to democracy.

In 2014 the Republic Earth journey will begin by encouraging citizens to be active democratic citizens by regularly voting on a range of hard and soft power issues. For example, people could vote on important global issues like eradicating poverty and taking action on climate change, as well as voting for their favourite song and film for 2014. Democracy does not just have to be political, it can be fun as well. For example, music could unite Republic Earth each year on New Year's Eve. Each year democracy could be used to determine the people's song for that year during New Year's Eve celebrations. Sydney, with its famous New Year's Eve fireworks, could lead the way and announce the winners each year. To find out more visit www.republicearth.org.

Republic Earth agrees with Moises Naim that 'we are on the verge of a revolutionary wave of positive political and institutional innovations', as a result of the More, Mobility and Mentality revolutions that have affected the world over the last two decades.[50] Greek democracy and the French Revolution led to a surge in radical and positive innovations in government but we are now overdue for another. As the historian Henry Steele Commager asserted about the eighteenth century:

---

[49]   'Computer Technologists Statement on Internet Voting', viewed on 16 August 2014 <https://www.verifiedvoting.org/projects/internet-voting-statement/>

[50]   Moises Naim, The End of Power: From Boardrooms to Battlefields & Churches to States, why being in charge isn't what it used to be, (Basic Books, New York, 2013), 238.

'We have invented practically every major political institution which we have, and we have invented none since. We have invented the political party and democracy and representative government. We invented the first independent judiciary in history ... We invented judicial review. We invented the superiority of the civil over the military power. We invented freedom of religion, freedom of speech, the Bill of Rights – well, we could go on and on ... Quite a heritage. But what have we invented since of comparable importance.'[51]

After World War II we did see the creation of the United Nations, the World Bank and the International Monetary Fund but the creation of an online democratic community called Republic Earth could be this new radical political innovation that the world is looking for and needs to deal with the challenges of the 21st century.

The digital revolution has allowed us to assemble en masse anywhere and, at the speed of light, connect to the world. This has opened up a new electronic frontier for freedom and democracy. According to Benjamin Barber, 'over a dozen years ago the still robust British charity Citizens Online proposed a "Civic Commons in Cyberspace" intended to realize democracy online ... Another British charity, UK Citizens Online Democracy (UKCOD), does similar work ... In France, Le World e.gov Forum [exists] ... [while] in the United States, the Benton Foundation's Digital Divide project' is trying to overcome the digital inequality around the world.[52] There is also 'Change.org' that allows people to create petitions,

---

[51]   Henry Steele Commager, quoted in Moyers, A World of Ideas: Conversations with Thoughtful Men & Women About American Life Today & the Ideas Shaping Our Future, 232.

[52]   Benjamin Barber, If Mayors Ruled the World: Dysfunctional Nations, Rising Cities, (Yale University Press, New Haven, London, 2013), 262-263.

'Causes.com' that allows you to support and create a cause and 'GlobalCitizen.org' that aims to encourage people to join the campaign for a world without extreme poverty by 2030. The leading non-governmental agency promoting democracy at present is the National Endowment of Democracy (NED) that was established in 1983 to promote democracy abroad. Although it began with very small budgets, the NED has given critical aid to democratic movements in Poland, Nicaragua, and Chile, as well as in many other countries. The work of the International Republican Institute also needs to be commended for their commitment to advancing freedom and democracy worldwide. Republic Earth wishes to build on these projects to encourage citizens of the world to join a global online democratic community called Republic Earth.

CHAPTER VI: THE REPUBLIC OF AUSTRALIA

Ω

'In this day and age, with all we've come to represent …
[it is still the case that we are] represented by the Queen
of Great Britain. What sort of fossilisation gets you
thinking in those terms? The fact is we need the republic
and we need it now. Not because of what it says to
others about us, but what it says to us about ourselves.
That's why we need it.'[53]

Paul Keating

On 6 November 1999 Australia held an Australian Republic Referendum. The aim for Australia was to move from a constitutional monarchy with an English monarch as head of state to an Australian republic with an Australian as head of state. The Australian Labor Party under the leadership of former Prime Minister Paul Keating had led this campaign for an Australian republic in the early 1990s; however, after the Keating Labor Government was defeated in 1996, Australians were denied a proper opportunity to become a republic due to the trickiness displayed by former conservative Prime Minister John Howard during the referendum. The Australian Republican Referendum of 1999 was ultimately unsuccessful and while conservative forces in Australia may continue to promote the virtues

---

[53]   Paul Keating, *After Words: Post-Prime Ministerial Speeches*, (Allen & Unwin, Sydney, 2011), 237.

of being beholden to the British monarchy, it is still the case that most Australians desire to complete the journey of becoming a truly independent nation by creating an Australian republic with an Australian as head of state.

In Australia it is the Australian people who decide our governments of the day and our prime ministers via democratically held elections. Queen Elizabeth II, our foreign British head of state, does not decide our governments or our prime ministers – it is the Australian people. Thus, in reality, the sovereignty of the nation is already in the hands of the Australian people and thus Australia is arguably a republic in all but name; however, officially Australia is still a constitutional monarchy whereby the sovereignty of the nation still resides with the English monarch, Queen Elizabeth II.

In 1999 during the Australian Republic Referendum, most Australians were in favour of Australia becoming a republic. However, John Howard complicated the question, and a simple vote on 'whether Australia should become a republic?' was not granted to the Australian people. If that simple vote had happened, then Australia may already be a republic. But instead, the Australian people struck down the republic model put before them in the 1999 referendum as 55 per cent of Australians voted no to Australia becoming a republic.[54] In the end, the 1999 Republican Referendum was a disaster and prevented Australia from reaching its full potential as a nation state. However, the 1999 Republic Referendum did point out one fact – that Australians have yet to be inspired or convinced

---

[54]   Barry Everingham, 'Another Australia Day without our own head of state', The Age 26 January 2009, Viewed on 29 January 2012 at http://www.theage.com.au/opinion/another-australia-day-without-our-own-head-of-state-20090125-7pfi.html

by any of the republican models put before them. On this point, retired High Court Judge and monarchist Michael Kirby has noted that 'why change a system that works'. However, this comment is not attuned to the voices of over 40 per cent of Australians who still desired a republic in 2011, according to a recent Newspoll.[55] The key now is to reignite the republican debate in Australia by encouraging Australians to think about what republican model they would prefer and what do they want for the head of state.

HEAD OF STATE MODELS

A. WHAT DO WE WANT OF OUR HEAD OF STATE?

The key focus is to have an Australian head of state, as it seems unacceptable for a foreign English monarch to be our head of state in the 21st century. Moreover, our foreign monarch is also the head of state for 15 other Commonwealth and United Nations countries. So it is time for Australia to accept that we are no longer a colony but an independent nation that wants to continue to establish our own identity and place in the world. Accordingly, we have to have an Australian as head of state, in order to improve our political system and have more pride in our leaders knowing that they are all Australians.

Currently, Australia has three political institutions or leaders that fill the hierarchy of our political system. At the top we have our head of state, our Queen of Australia, currently being filled by Queen Elizabeth II. Next in line is the Governor-General of Australia, currently being filled by Governor-General Peter Cosgrove. Finally, we have the Prime

---

[55] 'Republic' Newspoll published 27/04/11 viewed 9 January 2012 < http://www.newspoll.com.au/image_uploads/110402%20Republic.pdf>

Minister of Australia, currently being filled by Prime Minister Tony Abbott. For most republicans the fact that at the top of our political system we have a foreigner as head of state is totally unacceptable, so we should always ask, 'What do we want of our head of state?'

Flowchart A: Australia's Constitutional Monarchy

QUEEN OF AUSTRALIA
(Divine Right)
GOVERNOR-GENERAL
(Appointed by the Australian Government)
PRIME MINISTER OF AUSTRALIA
(Elected by the Australian People)

For Australia to progress we need to start thinking creatively about what Australia wants to be in the future and what our national values are. Do we want to continue with a foreign monarch or do we want to create institutions that inspire Australians and the rest of the world. England at the moment has two hierarchical political institutions, the Queen of England and the Prime Minister. Ireland also has two hierarchical political institutions, the President of Ireland and the Prime Minister of Ireland, both directly elected by its people. The United States has one political hierarchy institution, the President of the United States of America, currently being filled by President Barack Obama. This single political institution is the so called leader of the free world and has become both a popular hard and soft power symbol throughout the world. The common theme here is that each country throughout the world has developed its own hierarchical political institutions, including Australia. The key issue now for Australia is to start to imagine what it wants its new Australian head of state to be.

Hopefully, a future Australian republic will embrace Keating's 'vision of enlargement' whereby 'inside Australia, we must move further along the road of becoming one country and one economy and, outside it, an integral part of the region [and the world] around us.'[56] As Aboriginal academic Gregory Phillips notes, 'the Republic is our opportunity to dream, to remake and build the state we truly want', but we must make peace between Aboriginal peoples and the rest of the country before forming a new republic for all.[57]

B. MODEL 1: THE KEATING MINIMALIST MODEL - #K-ModelAusRepublic

For many Australian republicans, including long-time republican ambassador former Prime Minister Paul Keating, all they want is a minimalist change, where we reduce our three hierarchical political institutions to two, and simply make our Governor-General the head of state under a new title called the President of Australia. According to Keating, this new look President would be 'appointed by both houses of parliament, meaning by both major parties, while leaving the reserve powers with the new head of state as the Liberals had always wanted.'[58] This model is supported by many people, including *The Australian* journalist Greg Sheridan, who argues that a future Australian figurehead should not be elected.[59] This change would succeed in

---

56   Paul Keating, *After Words: Post-Prime Ministerial Speeches*, (Allen & Unwin, Sydney (2011), 118.

57   Gregory Phillips, 'Aboriginal Peoples & the Republic: A rationale for change', viewed 16 August 2014
      <http://wheelercentre.com/dailes/post/48726e394901>

58   Paul Keating, *After Words: Post-Prime Ministerial Speeches*, (Allen & Unwin, Sydney (2011), 60-61

59   Greg Sheridan, 'A Fighurehead should not be elected', *The Australian* 27 October 2011, 12.

fulfilling the objectives of the Australian Republican Movement; however, many Australians are not inspired by this form of change because the President of Australia would not be directly elected by the people.

Flowchart B: The Keating Model – #K-ModelAusRepublic

PRESIDENT OF AUSTRALIA
(Elected by Parliamentarians)
PRIME MINISTER OF AUSTRALIA
(Elected by the Australian People)

C.   MODEL 2: THE DIRECT ELECTION MODEL – #DE-ModelAusRepublic

The preferred model for the Australian people is to have an Australian head of state who is directly elected by the Australian people but would play the same role as our current Governor-General. The Australian people still want our Prime Minister to play the main hard power political role but would like an Australian head of state in the form of an Australian President who would play a soft power ceremonial role of advancing Australian national interest on the world stage.

Flowchart C: The Direct Election Model – #DE-ModelAusRepublic

PRESIDENT OF AUSTRALIA
(Elected by the Australian People)
PRIME MINISTER OF AUSTRALIA
(Elected by the Australian People)

D. MODEL 3: THE DEMOCRACY MODEL - #D-ModelAusRepublic

A third option for the Australian people to consider is the democracy model, as the Republic Earth ideology could be the inspiration needed to see Australia transition from a constitutional monarchy to an Australian republic. Australia is a modern democratic country with an ancient and continuous indigenous culture of over 40,000 years, and these two key features of Australia's national identity should be reflected in a future Australian republic. There should be a sense of dual sovereignty in a future Republic of Australia, where the new Australian constitution should maintain our current national parliament and the institution of the Prime Minister but also create a new Aboriginal autonomous parliament and a new Aboriginal and Torres Strait Islander leader called the Head of the Indigenous Peoples to represent the more than 670,000 indigenous people living in Australia. Australia should also acknowledge the genocide that occurred to our indigenous peoples and establish a Truth and Reconciliation Commission so we can deal with our past mistakes and move on to a brighter future.

In addition to embracing these two key features of Australia's identity, we should add a third pillar to a future Republic of Australia, which is to embrace democracy and be the nation that leads the world in creating this global, online democratic community called Republic Earth. Australia is a young nation state with its political mother being Great Britain and its older brother being the United States of America; however, it is unique, as it was the first country in the world to be created by a democratic vote in 1901 and is one of only 10 countries in the world where compulsory voting is enforced at elections.[60] On that note, Australia has an opportunity to advance the cause of democracy in the 21st century by establishing a new political institution or leader called a President of Australia that would act as a 'soft power' leader who would advance the cause of democracy for not only Australians but also for the rest of the world.

The key for Australia in transitioning to an Australian republic is to replace two of our outdated British hierarchical political institutions with new Australian made political figures. We will keep our Prime Minister who will continue to play the hard power political role for our country, but create new soft power political institutions that promote Australia's national interests. The Queen of Australia, Queen Elizabeth II, basically plays a soft power role in society, as the hard power role the British Kings and Queens once had is long gone (last time was prior to the 'Glorious Revolution' of 1688) and now the British Prime Minister is the most important political figure in the country. The same occurs in Australia; however, it is now time for Australia to create our very own soft power leaders and institutions to work in tandem with the Australian Prime Minister in the 21st century. American political scientist Joseph Nye pioneered the theory of soft power, and in the 21st century Australia can be a great soft power country by promoting the theory of Republic Earth that values all of humanity and by creating

---

[60] 'Compulsory Voting', viewed 16 August 2014
<http://en.m.wikipedia.org/wiki/Compulsory_voting>

new soft power leaders that inspire the world.[61] This book suggests we create the following three hierarchical political institutions:

i. President of Australia

First, at the top we should have a new head of state called the President of Australia who would have the same reserve powers and play much the same role as the current Governor-General but would have the new added role of advancing and defending the principle of democracy and creating a global online democratic community called Republic Earth.[62] The President of Australia should also develop a national commitment to the entire human family and all its cultures based on the Republic Earth ideology. However, unlike the Keating model's President, this democracy model President of Australia would be directly elected by a secret ballot using the Preferential System by a majority of Australians on a new look election day called 'Democracy Day' (see Democracy Day - Four Year Cycle) and

---

[61] Joseph Nye, Soft Power: The Means to Success in World Politics, (Public Affairs, 2005), 1.

[62] The functions and roles of the President of Australia would also include appointing ambassadors, ministers and judges, and being a guardian of democracy and to legislation, issuing writs for elections and bestowing honours. The President of Australia would also be President of the Federal Executive Council and Commander-in-Chief of the Australian Defence Force. After making changes to the Constitution, all these powers and all these posts are held under the authority of the Australian Constitution. Further, the President of Australia would act as vice-regal representative to the Australian Capital Territory. The Constitution would grant the President of Australia a wide range of powers, but in practice he or she follows the conventions of the Westminster system and (with rare exceptions) acts only on the advice of the Prime Minister of Australia or other ministers. The President of Australia would have a ceremonial role in swearing in and accepting the resignations of Members of Parliament. Also some people would say that creating the position of the President of Australia would conflict with the role of the President in the Senate, however there would be no conflict because in the United States they also have a bicameral system that has a President of the United States of America and a President of the Senate and their roles do not conflict.

would have a four year term (maximum of two terms). Only Australian citizens aged 18 or more may vote and the AEC will enable voters the option to vote for the President of Australia online, as countries like Brazil are already offering voters the chance to vote online. Candidates must be Australian citizens aged 18 or more.

This new President of Australia would be effectively known as the 'People's President', as the aim of the President of Australia would be to advance the principle of democracy throughout Australia and the rest of the world. According to The Economist Intelligence Unit's 'Democracy Index for 2012', Australia is currently ranked the sixth best democracy in the world and Norway is ranked first.[63] But arguably it is in the nature of Australians to be the best we can be, so when Australia is one of the oldest and most stable democracies in the world that has developed a successful multicultural, pluralistic and secular democracy as well, it only seems natural to create a political symbol that promotes and defends democracy. By creating this institution of the 'People's President' an Australian republic would be putting power in the hands of the people in a democratic fashion and not in the hands of some privileged elite like in a feudal monarchy. Thus, creating a modern, democratically elected Australian head of state will ensure that the new head of state has the consent of the Australian people, unlike what occurs at present.

---

[63]   Democracy Index 2012.

The President of Australia would also be granted a new democratic parliamentary role under a Republic of Australia. The President of Australia would be required to act as the 'People's President' during each sitting week whereby Australians would send questions to the President of Australia who would then ask them in parliament. During each sitting week the President of Australia would be required to ask questions to any of the members of the House of Representatives on Tuesday nights from 6 pm to 6.30 pm. This new Q&A feature will improve Australia's democracy and should be modelled on the concept created by Our Say.[64] Accordingly, the People's President would not be able to ask any personal questions but would be required to only ask the most popular questions as voted for under the Our Say system or via Republic Earth online democracy tool. This new Q&A special feature will make our democracy connect to the digital age and make our democracy one of the best in the world.

ii.   Head of the Indigenous Peoples

Secondly, Australia needs to develop a brand new institution or leader called the Head of the Indigenous Peoples or some more appropriate indigenous name. This new Head of the Indigenous Peoples or 'Leader' would have the role of advancing and protecting the interests of indigenous Australians and indigenous peoples across the globe. Since our colonial forbears reached our shores, the rich history of over 40,000 years of the indigenous Aboriginal people and Torres Strait Islanders has been devalued

---

[64]   Our Say', viewed on 29 January 2012 at http://www.oursay.org.au/the-australian-republic

and their human rights have been infringed. While we have made huge attempts as a nation to address our past wrongs and improve their standing in the community, it is important that we create an institution that will defend their interests for as long as humanity continues to exist. This Leader should also play a role of advancing the interests of the 370 million indigenous people in some 90 countries living throughout the world.[65] In doing so, this Leader should work in partnership with the United Nations Permanent Forum on Indigenous Issues that advises on issues such as indigenous economic and social development, culture, health and human rights.[66] Moreover, where there is a lack of global leader on indigenous issues it only seems natural for Australia to create a leader that defends their interests when we have one of the oldest continuing indigenous people living in our country. Furthermore, as the world increasingly becomes interconnected, it is more important than ever before to protect indigenous cultures and languages from becoming extinct, in order to ensure that the full richness of humanity is protected. Hence, creating both an Australian and a global ambassador for the indigenous peoples will be of great value to the world and

---

[65] United Nations Permanent Forum for Indigenous Peoples 2011, 'State Of the World's Indigenous Peoples', viewed 21 December 2011
http://www.un.org/esa/socdev/unpfii/en/spwip.html

[66] The Leader should also play a role in overseeing all government activity relating to the delivery of services to the 29 indigenous communities under the Remote Service Delivery National Partnership. This National Partnership was born out of Australia's 'Closing the Gap' initiative to reduce the gap between outcomes for indigenous and non-indigenous Australians.

Australians arguably would be extremely proud of Australia leading the way in the protection of indigenous peoples.

The Head of the Indigenous Peoples would be elected in a different year to the President of Australia (see Democracy Day - Four Year Cycle) but would be elected in the same manner as the President of Australia. For example, only Australian citizens aged 18 or more may vote and the AEC will enable voters the option to vote for the Head of the Indigenous Peoples online, and candidates must be Australian citizens aged 18 or more and do not need to be indigenous. This Leader would also play a similar parliamentary role as the President under a Republic of Australia, as this Leader, during each sitting week, would be required to ask questions to any senator in the Senate on behalf of the Australian people, on Thursday nights from 6 pm to 6.30 pm. Accordingly, just as the Senate protects the interests of smaller states and the proportional voting system protects the interests of minor parties, this Leader's role in leading a Q&A debate in the Senate would also make sure the interests of indigenous peoples continue to be heard.

This new Head of the Indigenous Peoples should also play the role of the leader in a new Aboriginal Parliament, which jointly negotiates with the Australian Federal Parliament. According to Gregory Phillips in his essay 'Aboriginal Peoples and the Republic', 'a trust fund of 2.5% of national GDP [should] be directed for autonomous management and control by the Aboriginal parliament for the maintenance of identity, land and cultures. Health education, housing, employment and justice programs for Aboriginal and Torres Strait Islander peoples should be directed by the Aboriginal and Torres Strait Islander Parliament.'[67] This will allow Australia's indigenous peoples to have some share power in the governing of the nation.

iii. Prime Minister of Australia

Finally, Australia would maintain the Prime Minister of Australia, as its foremost hierarchical political institution. In doing so we would continue to maintain our Westminster bicameral political system. The Prime Minister of Australia would continue to have the same powers and responsibilities, as they do at present. However, the Prime Minister of Australia would now be elected every four years by the Australian people (see Democracy Day - Four Year Cycle) and thus would no longer have the power to choose when to call an election, as elections would now be held on the last Saturday in November every four years.

Flowchart D: Democracy Model - #D-ModelAusRepublic

PRESIDENT OF AUSTRALIA
(Elected by the Australian People)
HEAD OF THE INDIGENOUS PEOPLES
(Elected by the Australian People)
PRIME MINISTER OF AUSTRALIA
(Elected by the Australian People)

---

[67] Gregory Phillips, 'Aboriginal Peoples & The Republic'.

Democracy Day - Four Year Cycle

Last Saturday in November

1st Year: Election of President of Australia

2nd Year: Federal Election

3rd Year: Election of Head of Indigenous Peoples

4th Year: Local Government Elections

*States/territories would choose when to hold their own elections.

**We should also have a new Australian flag and new national anthem representing the three new pillars of Australia mentioned above.

Since 1901 Australia has been in a process of severing our ties with Great Britain and forging its own identity. For example, in 1984 Australia decided to replace 'God Save the Queen' with 'Advance Australia Fair'. We have also sought to create our own political, economic, judicial and social institutions that are fully unique and independent. We have also witnessed Great Britain move away from us, for example, economically it decided to join the European Economic Community in 1973 and in the process severed many economic ties with Australia. Despite this progress of Australia wanting to form its own identity and Great Britain moving away from us, it is still the case that Australia has a foreign monarch as our head of state, Queen Elizabeth II. This reality needs to change and hopefully one of the above models or some other model will appeal to the Australian people and encourage them to demand that Australia become a republic. Republic Earth in 2014 will start this debate and invite Australian citizens to vote for their favourite republic model at www.republicearth.org.

CONCLUSION

Ω

Prospero:

'Our revels now are ended. These our actors,
As I foretold you, were all spirits, and
Are melted into air, into thin air:
And like the baseless fabric of this vision,
The cloud-capp'd tow'rs, the gorgeous palaces,
The solemn temples, the great globe itself,
Yea, all which it inherit, shall dissolve,
And, like this insubstantial pageant faded,
Leave not a rack behind. We are such stuff
As dreams are made on; and our little life
Is rounded with a sleep.'

The Tempest by William Shakespeare, Act 4, Scene 1, 148-158

Each person's voice will eventually fade and be rounded with a sleep, but in the 21st century it is vital that everybody's creative democratic voice is heard while they live and it is vital we create a Republic Earth, as that is when dreams are made. Former US President Franklin Delano Roosevelt once said that:

'Happiness lies not in the mere possession of money, it lies in the joy of achievement, in the thrill of creative effort.'[68]

On that note, it is vital for people all around the world to think creatively about our planet's future and the role as citizens we should play in the future. This Republic Earth ideology was also inspired by Ken Robinson's request for people to become more creative. According to Ken Robinson, the 'starting point is that everyone has huge creative capacities as a natural result of being a human being. The challenge is to develop them. A culture of creativity has to involve everybody, not just a select few.'[69] Hopefully this book has at the very least encouraged more people to be creative, and hopefully people will understand that the political ideology of 'Republic Earth' is about uncovering the amazing creativity potential of humanity through using democracy. Hopefully this book has also provided a new hope for Australia. So let's start to make history. Let's make the globally interconnected online democratic community of Republic Earth a reality.

REPUBLIC EARTH 21ST CENTURY CAMPAIGNS

The goal of this book is not the end of the conversation, but the beginning of a new campaign to create a democratic Republic Earth. We invite you to continue the discussion by joining the Republic Earth community at www.republicearth.org or follow us on Twitter @Republic_Earth and participate in our campaigns.

---

[68] Inaugural Speech of Franklin Delano Roosevelt, Given in Washington, D.C., 4th March 1933, viewed 16 August 2014 http://history.eserver.org/fdr-inaugural.txt>

[69] Ken Robinson, *Out of Our Minds: Learning to be Creative,* (Capstone Publishing Ltd, UK, 2011), 3.

- Republic Earth will campaign to encourage people to become citizens of the global online democratic community called Republic Earth. Citizens will be able to meet in circles to discuss issues and citizens will be encouraged to become candidates to take the lead on democratic issues. If a candidate develops a popular idea, then Republic Earth will promote the idea as a 'star' democratic idea.

- Republic Earth will use the 21st century to embark on a continual educational campaign to explain its ideology and advance democracy. Republic Earth will also promote the virtues of education, as democracy depends on citizens being educated so they can deliberate and debate an issue before determining their own vote.

- Republic Earth will campaign to establish a global democracy by the end of the century. This will mean each human being will need access to at least a smart phone device or the internet to connect with this global online democratic community called Republic Earth.

- Republic Earth will campaign for its education, social, political, economic and technological principles mentioned above to become globally relevant in the 21st century.

- Republic Earth would campaign for all nations in the 21st century to consider becoming full-fledged democracies and become republics where the sovereignty of the nation is in the hands of the people. Australia should start this campaign by transitioning to a Republic of Australia with an Australian head of state.

- Republic Earth understands that democracy alone is not enough and that a rules-based democracy needs to be developed in countries lacking a democratic political system at present. This includes ensuring the following in each country:

  - Freedom of information

  - Anti-corruption bodies

  - Ombudsman's office

  - Public audits

  - Parliamentary oversight committees

  - The judicial system

  - Economic regulatory institutions

  - The electoral commission

  - Non-governmental organisations

  - An independent media

  - A vigilant citizenry

ACKNOWLEDGMENTS

My deepest thanks go to my writing partner, brother and Co-founder of Republic Earth Andrew White, otherwise known as Archefusion. I must also thank my editing assistants including my mum, Mary White, my dad, David White, my brother Anthony White, Danny Pearson and Joshua Funder.

I also wish to thank the Australian Labor Party and the Labor for an Australian Republic Group for their support.

ACKNOWLEDGMENTS

Thank you to everyone who contributed to the initial productions of AN OCEAN IN MY SOUL, particularly Mary Schaugh for brilliantly directing the world premiere and the subsequent run the following month and Shon Le Blanc for providing costumes in a pinch. Thank you to Evelyn Rudie at the Santa Monica Playhouse team for betting on my work not once, but twice in less than a year. Thank you to my cast and crew members for pouring their hearts into this labor of love that had been such a long time coming. Thank you to my former NYU professor, Awam Amkpa, for the incredible course, Theater of the Black Atlantic, which inspired me to write this play as a final project in 2006. Thank you to my family and friends for the support and encouragement over the years. Thank you to my husband, Evan Malouf, for continuing to believe in me even when my own faith wavers. Thank you to my friends, family, and colleagues who came to experience the magic in person. Thank you to Dorea Slagle, Alexis Ingram, and Mixed Magic Theatre for keeping momentum going with innovative online productions when theaters everywhere were closing their doors in 2020 due to COVID. Thank you to the audiences at the Santa Monica Playhouse in 2019 for supporting live theater and opening your hearts afterwards, the stories you shared still touch me to this very day. Thank you to everyone who reads AN OCEAN IN MY SOUL and brings it to life again and again.

WORLD PREMIERE
CAST

Alexander .... Gilbert Roy

Omni .... Shawn Richardz

Colonist .... Jeremiah Benjamin

Gilbert .... Disraeli Ellison

Susan .... Janelle Poirier

Lydia .... Joslyn Beard

Malcolm .... Vincent J. Isaac

Bodies .... Janine Montag
Salwa Abussabur
Sakina Ibrahim

Written by Charise Sowells
Directed by Mary Schaugh
Choreographed by Sakina Ibrahim
Produced by Charise Sowells
Costumes by Shon Le Blanc
Score by Charise Sowells
Stage Manager: Asia Turner
Technical Director: Evelyn Rudie

Brought to you by Unabashed Productions and The
Binge Fringe Fest.

Santa Monica Playhouse, Santa Monica, CA, USA,
October, 2019

ENCORE RUN
CAST

Alexander .... Gilbert Roy

Omni .... Matt Jennings

Colonist .... Jeremiah Benjamin

Gilbert ....…..….…. Disraeli Ellison

Susan .... Janelle Poirier

Lydia ....…..…….… Joslyn Beard

Malcolm .... Vincent J. Isaac

Bodies ....…...Tenika Pouncie
Tiara T. Hairston
Kaeche Libra

Written by Charise Sowells
Directed by Mary Schaugh
Choreographed by Tenika Pouncie
Produced by Charise Sowells
Costumes by Shon Le Blanc
Score by Charise Sowells
Stage Manager: Asia Turner
Technical Director: George J. Vennes III

Brought to you by Unabashed Productions and
Santa Monica Playhouse Benefit Series.

Santa Monica Playhouse, Santa Monica, CA, USA,
November, 2019

AN OCEAN IN MY SOUL
By Charise Sowells

CHARACTERS

Alexander, teens, an introspective Multiracial boy torn between worlds

Omni, narrator, the voice of history lost

Colonist, 40's, stout and self-content European man for whom business always comes first

Gilbert, 40's, slow-moving gentle Black man with an idealistic heart

Susan, 30's, tenderhearted White woman who means well and wants the best for her son

Lydia, 30's, graceful nurturing Black woman, a warrior through and through

Malcolm, 60's, insightful elderly Black man who tells it like it is

Bodies, personification of the waves of the black Atlantic

WRITER'S NOTE

The song "I've Got Peace Like a River" is a song enslaved African Americans wrote and sang. The title of this one-act play comes from a line in the song but all other words in the script are indigenous to my imagination.

SCENE 1

The stage is moving like a black ocean. In the water heads and limbs bob up and down. The moon shines full and bright in the distance. An omniscient voice booms after a moment or two.

OMNI: Bobbing in this sea of transnational beings. Trying to keep our heads above the water which has stolen so much of our past. We are united by our displacement:

Black, African, mixed, gay, Afro-Asian Brits, indigenous people and all people marginalized in societies everywhere. Due to the recklessness of colonization and slavery, indentured servitude and forced migration, mixed breeding of people like dogs and the destruction of cultures and lands for economic profits.

To all of you who have suffered through the repercussions of these movements: <u>this is our home</u>. How, you may ask, is this sea darkened by our bloody histories anything one might call a home?

It is the one location that binds us and keeps us strong when the rest of the world weakens us and detaches us from who we are and where we came from. It is a way to hold on to what has been thrashed and torn to pieces for centuries.

This ocean of memories is the Black Atlantic. The one place we can always refer back to so that we may never forget the sacrifices of our ancestors. Instead we shall remember the community of which we are a part and know that we are never alone in our struggle... Welcome home.

The water begins to boil furiously taking the heads below the surface. A ship roles in. Most importantly the grand sails move across the water. COLONIST, a jovial European man quite satisfied with himself, walks on stage in front of the water and stands with scroll in hand. Spotlight on him.

COLONIST: Hello, you savage beasts. Please, do be kind and pay us mind for only a moment. This land you have is quite lovely, I must say. If only it were to remain your land forever. *(Laughs)* The time has come for you to evolve into a civilized existence with a civilized language and a civilized belief system.

Most importantly, you are in dire need of a civilized economy with monetary values and hierarchy. Do you understand? You will thank us for this later, I promise. Your land will be more prosperous than you ever fathomed possible!

We ask for your cooperation, oh who am I kidding? You will cooperate with us or face the consequences. Those being a slow and painful death, a breaking down of your spirits, a raping of your most prized women oh and, just for fun the stealing of your children. We will do our best to keep your families together but at this point you are seen as part of the land and will be treated thusly.

Any questions? Of course not, you don't understand a word I'm saying, do you? Well, isn't that grand. Please, sign here, my friends and submit your lives to our hands.

*The Colonist offers his scroll and a feather pen to
the audience with a Cheshire Cat smile. Spotlight
off.*

SCENE 2

*On the other side of the stage GILBERT and LYDIA, a
black man and woman sit. The mother cradles the baby to
her breast. Soft light shines upon them. The baby is lighter in
complexion than the both of them.*

GILBERT: He's quiet now.

LYDIA: He was just hungry.

GILBERT: I don't want him to go.

LYDIA: It's not up to us, Gilbert. You know that.

GILBERT: I do. That doesn't mean I like it.

Pause.

LYDIA: I don't like it much either. He's my baby no
matter how he came to be. He's my only one... But
he's going to have a good life. Better than the life we
could give him.

GILBERT: He's gonna be telling us what to do out
there like that man Neil is now. Yellin' at us all the
time like he forgot where he came from. He's gonna
forget who he is too, they all do.

LYDIA: Not if I have anything to do with it. They
might take him away but he's still my little boy.

GILBERT: I love him like he's my own child too, Lydia. I don't know why but I do.

LYDIA: Because you love me, that's why.

GILBERT: I suppose that's true.

They kiss.

GILBERT: I gotta get back to work now. You better hurry up too before Masta' gets mad.

LYDIA: I'm feeding his baby for god's sake.

GILBERT: Don't make no difference to him, Lydia.

He puts his hat on.

GILBERT: I'd say you don't got much more than five minutes before he comes out lookin' for you.

He exits.

LYDIA: You finished yet baby Alex? Mama's gotta get back to work. Ya hear?

Baby Alex continues nursing. She begins rocking him.

LYDIA: You sure are beautiful, you know that? Amazing something so beautiful can come from what I went done through. I wouldn't take it back if I could now. Didn't think I wanted it at the time, I was screaming for my life. But insteada' listening to me, God gave me you…

A combination of joyful and bitter tears fall from her eyes. Baby Alex begins to cry too. She lightly caresses him, shushing him.

LYDIA: Now just because I'm crying doesn't mean you need to start. Mama's alright, Alexander. Mama's gonna be alright.

She hums a lullaby. Begin Song, "Enter Your Dreams".

LYDIA *(singing):* LISTEN QUIETLY
BE STILL AND YOU'LL SEE
ALL IS CALM HERE
CLOSE YOUR EYES
AND ENTER YOUR DREAMS
LALALA

End Song. Alex is finally asleep. She carries him off stage to put him to bed. Lights out.

SCENE 3

An older ALEXANDER walks onto the other side of the stage. Grown up and dressed more like the Colonist than his parents, he carries a whip. Following after him is the Colonist.

COLONIST: I think you've been doing a mighty fine job up until this point, Alexander. Do not disappoint me now. I'm relying on you to make sure that this plantation runs properly and if that means beating those niggers until they ain't got no more power to say anything about it then that's what I expect you to do.

ALEXANDER: Yes, masta'.

COLONIST: You may not think that I understand what's going on here but I see it all clear as day. You feel sympathetic for that negress who gave birth to you but she is not your mother anymore. She is no different than the rest of them niggers out there, she is beneath you. Does she feed you?

ALEXANDER: Not any more, masta'.

COLONIST: No, she doesn't. And she barely gave you food when she had you. She gave you what was in her breasts and once that ran dry we took you into our home and raised you up in our house so you were strong and healthy like a good overseer should be. Now look at your clothes and look at all the poor niggers out there who got nothing to wear but the shirt on their backs. Is that what you want?

ALEXANDER: No, masta.

COLONIST: No is right. You want the life we can give you. And we want you to have that life too, son. So you just do your job and you'll get to keep this life.

ALEXANDER: Yes, masta'.

COLONIST: That a boy. Now how many lashings does Miss Lydia get? Do you remember?

ALEXANDER: Yes, sir. 40 lashings masta'.

COLONIST: That's right. 10 for every minute she was late to her shift on the field, and she knows that by now so don't take pity on her. Personally I hate to see a creature as pretty as she is get hurt at all, but pretty a negress as she may be, she's still a negress and must obey our rules. I'll tie her up for ya and see to it that she's in place for her whipping. When you hear me holler, you come on down and finish her off.

ALEXANDER: Yes, masta'.

COLONIST: Course you might hear her scream first, but pay no mind to that. I'm just reminding her who's boss. *(Laughs)*

Colonist exits. Alexander looks out. The screams of his mother come from the other side of the stage in the darkness. Tears fill Alex's eyes.

The water begins to move again. The heads and limbs begin to bob. They chant with growing volume, Begin Song "Remember Who You Are".

BODIES *(singing): ALEX, REMEMBER,*
REMEMBER WHO YOU ARE
ALEX, REMEMBER,
BEFORE YOU GO TOO FAR
ALEX, REMEMBER,
REMEMBER WHO YOU ARE

End Song. Alex falls to his knees and prays to the omniscient. Begin Song, "Dear God".

ALEXANDER *(singing): DEAR GOD,*
CAN YOU HEAR ME?
CAN YOU SEE ME ON MY KNEES?
DEAR GOD, NOW I NEED YOU
I'VE BEEN LIVING FAITHFULLY
DEAR GOD, I NEED SAVING
FROM THIS MOMENT IN MY LIFE

COLONIST: Alexander!

ALEXANDER *(singing)*: *DEAR GOD,*
I'M AFRAID YOU
HAVE FORSAKEN ME THIS TIME

End Song. The water begins to settle. Begin Song,
"Remember Who You Are Reprise".

BODIES *(singing)*: *ALEX, REMEMBER,*
BEFORE YOU GO TOO FAR

End Song. The ocean is still. We hear the mother
whimpering. Alex stands slowly getting himself together and
picking up his whip, walking into the darkness.

SCENE 4

Daytime. The ocean has absorbed into the field. Gilbert and
MALCOLM are picking cotton. Alex is in the
background, overseeing.

MALCOLM: Does the masta' know she's not
workin'?

GILBERT: No, and that's how it needs to stay.

MALCOLM: You know, if a son of mine ever did
that to me I wouldn't have no more reason to get
out of bed in the morning.

GILBERT: Seems like she feels the same way. It's
not like she never been whipped before. But this
time, it seemed to cripple her before the whip even
grazed her skin. The minute she saw Alex draw back
his hand...she was gone. I never seen her eyes so
empty.

MALCOLM: He's a nasty negro he is, to do that to his mama.

GILBERT: He don't have no choice.

MALCOLM: We all got a choice. If I had to risk my life or my mama's I would choose mine. That's a choice. And he chose his mother's.

GILBERT: Either way, Lydia didn't bring him into this world to have him taken away. She is real sympathetic to his situation. She'll love that boy till the day she dies.

MALCOLM: It's a shame the way this happens. The masta' just goes around causin' trouble every way he can and leaves the mess for everybody else to clean up after.

GILBERT: What are you talkin'?

MALCOLM: He rapes our women, then steals our children and turns 'em all against us. Every one of 'em. Mulattoes are the most selfish people out there. They don't care about the masta', don't care about the slaves, all they care about is themselves or they wouldn't go around beatin' everything that moved.

GILBERT: Alex don't do that.

MALCOLM: Well, he's new blood. Give him a couple more years and you'll see. You won't even want to call him family no more, you'll be too ashamed to.

GILBERT: I ain't never gonna disown my son the way he has me and Lydia. What right would I have to be hurting right now if I planned on hurtin' him the same way?

MALCOLM: Well, now, I hate to say this Gilbert but he ain't your son.

GILBERT: What is Lydia's is mine, Malcolm. Nothin's gonna change that.

MALCOLM: You know, I've been on this here plantation longer than you and Lydia have put together. Maybe you don't wanna hear what I got to say now, but you'll remember this conversation years down the road and wish you'da listened to me.

GILBERT: Just because I don't agree, don't mean I'm not listenin'.

Pause. Alex clears his throat. Malcolm takes off his hat and rubs his face.

MALCOLM: It's a hot one today, ain't it?

GILBERT: Sure is.

A wave from the black Atlantic washes over Alex from behind. Gilbert and Malcolm look back as the wave engulfs them too. Lights out.

SCENE 5

The moon rises once again. The heads and limbs bob. The omniscient voice booms.

OMNI: Now we travel to an Alexander of another time. Mixed and confused, resented by his peers, he is accepted as an exception to blackness in the white

world. He is dismissed for his shortcomings of blackness in the black world. Instead of being treated as both he is perceived as neither.
There is no happy medium between his two halves. Circumstances are not as devastating as they were for the biracial overseers, but are complicated nonetheless. And because of this Alex clings fervently to the ocean floor just hoping to find footing on a piece of common ground.

The ocean rises to reveal Alex amidst the other bodies in the ocean. He is wandering. The bodies touch him, pull him aside, make him listen and interact when they are talking.

BODY 1: Look at his skin. It's so pretty. I love those light skinned boys. Too bad he doesn't have the light eyes and hair too. That's the ideal mix.

BODY 2: I bet he doesn't even go for sistas. He probably thinks he's too good for us. Well, guess what then, we're too good for you. You don't even dress right.

BODY 3: You know what I like about you Alexander? You don't have that obnoxious blaccent. You know what I mean? That like ghetto, "Yo, I'm a thug so watch out," talk. It's like, oh please. Get a job and grow up.

BODY 1: I love that hair. It's so big. How did you get it like that? Is it natural?

BODY 2: Oh, so you act white like that cuz you're mixed? Well, that's cool. We'll just have to help you out, get you some corn rows or somethin'. Teach you how to walk with swagger and everythang.

BODY 3: Diversity and tolerance. We are all about mixing it up and letting all kinds of people work for us. It looks good on our part now a days anyway. And what's great about you is that you can really go either way.

BODY 1: I love how universal you look. It's so in right now.

BODY 2: Boy, you got good hair! You should straighten it. *(Yanks Alex's head back)*

BODY 1: One more question before you go. What's up with your hair? I know it's not a Jew fro but what is it? Don't worry, this won't affect the hiring decision.

BODY 3: I love dating you. But you know I could never bring you home to meet my family, right?

ALEXANDER: Stop it! All of you! I want to go home.

The ocean sinks and a projection of home lights its surface.

OMNI: Home.
What is home?
Is it the house you grew up in?
Is it the town you learn to love
after finally managing to move away?
Is it a safe space
where no one challenges
or invalidates your existence?
Is home in the people who love you?
Is home inside?
Is home ever-changing with the tide?

Home light off.

SCENE 6

A light comes up on the forefront of the stage. Alexander enters. His mom, SUSAN, is on the other side cooking. She is white.

SUSAN: Oh, you're home.

ALEXANDER: Yeah.

SUSAN: How was your day?

ALEXANDER: Fine.

SUSAN: Fine? That's it?

No response.

SUSAN: Did something happen?

ALEXANDER: No, I'm just sick of dealing with this.

SUSAN: Dealing with what, Alex?

ALEXANDER: Just everyone telling me what I can and can't be.

SUSAN: They're jealous, honey.

ALEXANDER: No, they're not jealous Mom.

SUSAN: Why do you think they say the things they do, because they feel good about themselves

ALEXANDER: I donno.

SUSAN: Well, I know.

ALEXANDER: You don't know anything about being mixed.

SUSAN: I've raised you haven't I? When you were little I dealt with people constantly asking me if you were adopted. People I didn't even know believed they had the right to ask me anything they wanted. Why? Because they're so unsure of the world that they want people like you and me to clarify and make things easier for them.

ALEXANDER: That doesn't mean they're jealous.

SUSAN: Okay, jealous may not be the best word. But insecure. That's what they are. And you know what, some of them are jealous too.

ALEXANDER: That's such a mom response.

SUSAN: What do you mean?

ALEXANDER: You always make it seem like everything is other people's problems, not mine.

SUSAN: Well, it is their problem that they don't understand you. They're ignorant.

ALEXANDER: Who's ignorant Mom? The whole world?

SUSAN: Unless they've had some experience with this issue, yes. I would say so.

ALEXANDER: I'm just so sick of people asking me "What are you?" or "Why do you talk so white?" It's like, why do you need to know?

SUSAN: I know, it's not easy-

ALEXANDER *(overlapping)*: No, you don't know, Mom. And neither does Dad.

SUSAN: We do know Alex because the people that are confused or bothered by you are the same people who give me and your father dirty looks when we walk down the street together. Your father and I have been through a hell of a lot more than you realize, merely because we loved each other during an era when racism was still very much alive.

My own family nearly disowned me until the day I told them I was pregnant with you. They thought I had betrayed the family and settled for less but little did they know that your father had more love in his heart for me than my family ever did. He didn't judge me. He didn't see my color. He believed in my dreams and I knew he would make the best father a child could have.

She collapses in a chair at the table. Pause.

ALEXANDER: Are you okay?

SUSAN: No, Alex. I don't like to see you go through this. You'd think people would have wised up by now and gotten over themselves enough to realize people are people. Each and every one of us and race is just something society want us to live by. It's not even real. I'm no different than your father. You're no different than us. We're human.

ALEXANDER: Yeah, I wish it didn't matter.
But it does, Mom.

SUSAN: Well, thankfully you have nice friends.
Right? That little mixed girl that you hang out with
is so cute. You two almost look like siblings.

ALEXANDER: Mom.

SUSAN: What? With the hair and you two basically
have the same skin tone. You don't think so?

ALEXANDER: Yeah, we're both brown with big
hair but that's it. She doesn't look like my sister.

Alex goes to the table.

SUSAN: All I'm saying is that she's a nice girl and
you two have an understanding. You should be
thankful. Your experience is unique, you know? Not
just anyone can grasp the things you go through and
having someone that does because they've been
through it too is invaluable. That's why I go to my
women's group.

ALEXANDER: Is being a woman really that hard?

SUSAN: Yes, in fact it is sometimes, Alex. Men
don't understand women the way other women do
and it's nice to know I'm not the only one that feels
that way.

Pause.

ALEXANDER: What are you making for dinner?

SUSAN: Chicken Parm. Why don't you help me finish setting the table? It's almost ready.

He goes to the drawer and gets some silverware.

ALEXANDER: You know, I'm thinking about studying African American History next year.

SUSAN: When did you make that decision?

ALEXANDER: We just had this chapter on slavery in my history class and I donno, I think it's good to know that stuff.

SUSAN: Your dad never found any purpose for it.

ALEXANDER: I'm not Dad. I want to know where I came from.

SUSAN: You came from us.

ALEXANDER: Right. But before that. I think it's important. Maybe if everyone knew their history they would stop hating people for no reason. Maybe we would understand everyone more and just see each other as people, you know?

SUSAN: African American History is only a part of your history, Alex.

ALEXANDER: I know, but it's a part school always leaves out. And I'm sick of feeling like I don't know who I am.

SUSAN: Well, I know who you are. You're my beautiful baby boy and I love you just the way you are.

ALEXANDER: I know.

SUSAN: Your grandmother always worried about how difficult your life would be. I thought she was being ridiculous at the time... Alex, I know you're going through a rough time but I want you to know that your father and I raised you the way we did so that you never have to pick sides.

ALEXANDER: Everybody else keeps picking sides for me.

SUSAN: That doesn't mean that you have to agree with them.

ALEXANDER: One drop, Mom.

SUSAN: What do you mean when you say that?

ALEXANDER: One drop of Black blood and I'm Black. That's it.

SUSAN: I don't like where this conversation is going.

ALEXANDER: That's the way it is, Mom.

He finishes setting the table.

ALEXANDER: Is dinner done yet?

SUSAN: Yes, but we're going to wait for your father to get home.

ALEXANDER: I'll be in my room.

SUSAN: Alex.

ALEXANDER: What?

SUSAN: This is the last thing I ever wanted to happen.

ALEXANDER: Why?

SUSAN: Because you're not black, you're mixed. And that's a beautiful thing. I don't want you to be ashamed of that, or in denial. It is who you are.

ALEXANDER: It's what I am. Who I am is what I'm trying to figure out.

Gilbert enters, Alex's dad.

SUSAN: Oh, honey. I'm glad your home.

GILBERT: Me too.

He kisses her on the cheek.

GILBERT: It was a long day. How you doin' there, kiddo?

ALEXANDER: I'm alright.

GILBERT: Alright?

SUSAN: He had a rough day today.

GILBERT: Is that right? You wanna talk about it?

ALEXANDER: It wasn't even like anything happened. I just got frustrated.

GILBERT: Frustrated? Frustrated about what?

ALEXANDER: I donno.

GILBERT: Don't say those words unless you *really* don't know, Alexander.

ALEXANDER: I don't. I just feel like I don't really belong anywhere.

GILBERT: Don't we all feel like that in high school? Didn't you, Susan?

SUSAN: Yes.

GILBERT: I did too. I swear that's what high school is for, making everyone feel like they're a misfit. But go on.

ALEXANDER: Forget it.

GILBERT: Good. And *you* should forget it too. Don't let those kids get to you, alright?

ALEXANDER: Yup.

SUSAN: You know he's thinking about taking African American History classes.

GILBERT: Good for you. They didn't even offer that when I was in school. How things have changed, huh?

Pause.

GILBERT: How's dinner coming along, Suze?

SUSAN: Ready when you are, Gil.

GILBERT: Ready? I'm famished.

SUSAN: Me too.

She puts the food on the table.

GILBERT: Grab a seat, Alex.

ALEXANDER: I'm not really hungry.

Alexander gets up from the table.

GILBERT: What do you mean you're not hungry? Did you eat? I'm talking to you!

Alex leaves. Gilbert looks at Susan in disbelief.

GILBERT: What is going on with him?

Susan shakes her head.

GILBERT: You took the time to cook us dinner and he's not even considerate enough to sit and eat it with us, let alone say thank you.

Gilbert puts down his napkin and moves to get up and go after Alex. Susan puts her hand on him.

SUSAN: It's okay. He's having a bad day. Let him be.

Both seated again now, they hold hands for a moment and then begin to eat. End Scene.

SCENE 7

Spotlight on Alexander on the other side of the stage.

ALEXANDER: Mongrels. Mulattoes. Mestizos.
Mutts.
All names for people like me everywhere.
We fall between the cracks, always lodged in
the middle of two opposing worlds.
Always questioned.
Usually misunderstood.
I want to know my history and grab a hold of me.
Who I am.
Not who someone believes me to be.
My feelings are valid.
My issues are real.
I deserve to be recognized for the person that I am.
Alexander Eugene Sanders.
Multiracial and proud!
You cannot shame me for existing.
I am as much a product of our history as all of you.
I deserve to know my roots.

The lights go out.

SCENE 8

The moon rises in the back. Heads and limbs bob in the ocean again. Omni sings. Begin Song, "Peace Like A River".

OMNI *(singing)* : *I'VE GOT PEACE LIKE A RIVER*
I'VE GOT PEACE LIKE A RIVER
I'VE GOT PEACE LIKE A RIVER IN MY SOUL
I'VE GOT JOY LIKE A FOUNTAIN
I'VE GOT JOY LIKE A FOUNTAIN
I'VE GOT JOY LIKE A FOUNTAIN IN MY SOUL

I'VE GOT LOVE LIKE AN OCEAN
I'VE GOT LOVE LIKE AN OCEAN
I'VE GOT LOVE LIKE AN OCEAN IN MY
SOUL

The bodies join in song along with the rest of the cast, even those behind the curtain.

EVERYBODY *(singing)* : *I'VE GOT PEACE LIKE A RIVER*
I"VE GOT PEACE LIKE A RIVER
I'VE GOT PEACE LIKE A RIVER IN MY
SOUL
I'VE GOT JOY LIKE A FOUNTAIN
I'VE GOT JOY LIKE A FOUNTAIN
I'VE GOT JOY LIKE A FOUNTAIN IN MY
SOUL
I'VE GOT LOVE LIKE AN OCEAN
I'VE GOT LOVE LIKE AN OCEAN
I'VE GOT LOVE LIKE AN OCEAN IN MY
SOUL

Lights come up on Lydia. Gilbert is applying meat fat to her wounds from the lashing.

GILBERT *(singing)* : *I'VE GOT LOVE LIKE AN OCEAN*
I'VE GOT LOVE LIKE AN OCEAN
I'VE GOT LOVE LIKE AN OCEAN IN MY
SOUL

End song. He laughs lightly.

GILBERT: Remember that one?

LYDIA *(weakly)*: How could I forget?

GILBERT: I used to sing him to sleep with that one. And I meant it too. I really did love him with my whole heart. It just flowed out of me. 'Course I never could have loved him the way you did, Lydia. But I loved him more than I woulda' ever known a man could love if he hadn't come into our lives.

He finishes with her wounds.

GILBERT: There you go.

LYDIA: Thank you, Gilbert.

GILBERT: Now you let that sit in for a while before you get dressed. I know you hate to stay still for too long but you're just gonna have to. *(beat)* I would do anything I could for you, Lydia. I know Alex would too if his life weren't on the line.

LYDIA: I'd rather not talk about him, Gilbert. He's not my son anymore.

GILBERT: You don't mean that, Lydia.

LYDIA: Yes, I do. If he can do this to the woman who brought him into this world, then I am nothing to him. He wouldn't be alive if it wasn't for me. And now he's trying to take my life!

GILBERT: He had to do it. You know he don't got no say in the matter.

LYDIA: I would never lay a finger on him that didn't have love in its bones. Never.

GILBERT: I know, Lydia. You were good to him. We were both good to him.

LYDIA: Do you think he even remembers? Do you think he knows that we're his parents?

GILBERT: Yes. I do think so.

LYDIA: I just don't understand. I've never been so hurt in my life.

She leans on him.

GILBERT: Wounds within our hearts bring on the most pain.

He holds Lydia, rocking her like a baby.

GILBERT: I tell you one thing. I know his heart is hurtin' too. This is a bad for all of us. But this will pass. All things do. This will pass with the rest of them, Lydia. You'll see.

Lights fade on them. The ocean moves and sings one last time, softly. BODIES sing the "Peace Like a River Reprise". Begin Song.

BODIES *(singing)*: *I'VE GOT PEACE LIKE A RIVER*
I"VE GOT PEACE LIKE A RIVER
I'VE GOT PEACE LIKE A RIVER IN MY SOUL
I'VE GOT JOY LIKE A FOUNTAIN
I'VE GOT JOY LIKE A FOUNTAIN
I'VE GOT JOY LIKE A FOUNTAIN IN MY SOUL
I'VE GOT LOVE LIKE AN OCEAN
I'VE GOT LOVE LIKE AN OCEAN
I'VE GOT LOVE LIKE AN OCEAN IN MY SOUL

End Song. The water settles. The moon goes down below the horizon.

THE END

ABOUT THE PLAY

An Ocean In My Soul is a one-act play written by Charise Sowells about a multiracial teen who is torn between worlds that span time and space, united by the waves of the Black Atlantic. It had a sold out world premiere at the Santa Monica Playhouse in 2019. The following month, another successful run took place at the same theater with a few new cast members and different choreography. In addition to writing the script, Charise Sowells composed the score, painted the poster, and produced the shows. Both runs were directed by Mary Schaugh. Subsequent online productions took place; one was directed by Alexis Ingram in association with Mixed Magic Theater and the other was directed by Dorea Slagle. Shortly thereafter, the play was featured on a Radio Reverb show in the UK and added to a collection of plays for decolonizing theater classrooms put together by Momentum Stage.

AN OCEAN IN MY SOUL

Published by Unabashed Productions in December of 2025.

PRODUCTIONS

ONE-ACT PLAY - DRAMA

Synopsis: A multiracial teen is torn between worlds spanning
time and space, united by the waves of the Black Atlantic.
Run Time: 45 minutes.

WORLD PREMIERE: Santa Monica Playhouse

OCTOBER 25TH 2019

SOLD OUT: First show of the festival to fill all the seats.

ENCORE RUN: Santa Monica Playhouse

NOVEMBER 25TH & 26TH, 8PM

2019

ETC.

RADIO EXCERPT & INTERVIEW: Radio Reverb's
Sapphic Voices JULY 5TH 2020

ONLINE PRODUCTION: International Cast and Crew
APRIL 24TH 2020

COLLECTION: *Decolonizing The Classroom* For Teachers
MOMENTUM STAGE 2020

ONLINE PRODUCTION: Mixed Magic Theater APRIL
7TH 2020

READING: VS Theater/InkWell JANUARY 15TH 2020

CONTEST: ScreenCraft Stage Play Semifinalist 2020

PRESS

Broadway World, Theater Mania, Better Lemons, LAFPI,
The Grunion, Evensi, Downtown Santa Monica,
SantaMonica.com, Performing Arts LIVE, Mixed Race
Studies, Caffeinated Cinema

UNABASHED PRODUCTIONS

Don't just think outside the box, live there.

www.ingramcontent.com/pod-product-compliance
Lightning Source LLC
Chambersburg PA
CBHW052143270326
41930CB00012B/2997